Cheetahs

Cheetahs

by Dianne M. MacMillan

photographs by Gerry Ellis

A Carolrhoda Nature Watch Book

Carolrhoda Books, Inc. / Minneapolis

To my dear friend Hope, who is my
inspiration   —D. M. M.

This book is dedicated to the courage, will,
and indefatigable efforts of the Cheetah
Conservation Fund, co-founded by Laurie Marker-
Kraus and Dan Kraus, which fights
to keep the cheetah from becoming another
footnote to extinction.   —G. E.

Thanks to Susan Millard, associate researcher at the San Diego
Wild Animal Park; Judy Zeno, education curator at Wildlife
Safari; and Dr. Lindsey Phillips, School of Veterinary Medicine
at the University of California, Davis. Special thanks to Jack
Grisham, general curator at the Oklahoma City Zoological Park
and coordinator of the Species Survival Plan.

This book is available in two editions:
Library binding by Carolrhoda Books, Inc.
Soft cover by First Avenue Editions
c/o The Lerner Publishing Group
241 First Avenue North, Minneapolis, MN 55401 U.S.A.

LIBRARY OF CONGRESS CATALOGING-IN-PUBLICATION DATA

MacMillan, Dianne M., 1943–
    Cheetahs / by Dianne M. MacMillan; photographs by Gerry
Ellis.
        p.   cm.
    "A Carolrhoda nature watch book."
    Includes index.
    Summary: Describes the physical characteristics, life cycle,
behavior, and conservation of cheetahs.
    ISBN 1-57505-044-7 (lib. bdg.)
    ISBN 1-57505-225-3 (pbk.)
    1. Cheetah — Juvenile literature. [1. Cheetah.
2. Endangered species.] I. Ellis, Gerry, ill. II. Title.
QL737.C23M362 1997
599.74'428 — dc20   96-28554

Manufactured in the United States of America
1 2 3 4 5 6 – JR – 02 01 00 99 98 97

CONTENTS

In the cool early morning, a herd of antelope moves slowly across the African plain. The animals graze, unaware that on a distant mound two amber eyes watch their every move. Suddenly through the tall grass, a blur of spotted tan fur springs toward the herd. A large cat singles out one of the animals. Although the herd scatters, within seconds the hunter has caught and killed the antelope. The large cat is a cheetah, the fastest animal on land.

With long legs, a slender body, and beautiful spots, the cheetah is considered by many to be the most elegant of cats. Cheetahs are members of the cat family, called Felidae. All cats are part of this family—"big cats," such as lions, tigers, leopards, and jaguars, as well as house cats. The cheetah's scientific name is *Acinonyx jubatus*.

The cheetah (far right) *is smaller and more slender than its relatives the black leopard* (top), *the lion* (near right), *and the Siberian tiger* (bottom).

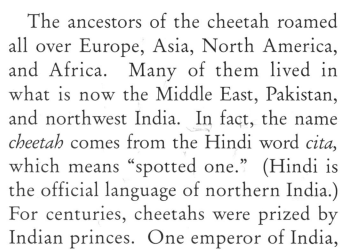

The ancestors of the cheetah roamed all over Europe, Asia, North America, and Africa. Many of them lived in what is now the Middle East, Pakistan, and northwest India. In fact, the name *cheetah* comes from the Hindi word *cita*, which means "spotted one." (Hindi is the official language of northern India.) For centuries, cheetahs were prized by Indian princes. One emperor of India,

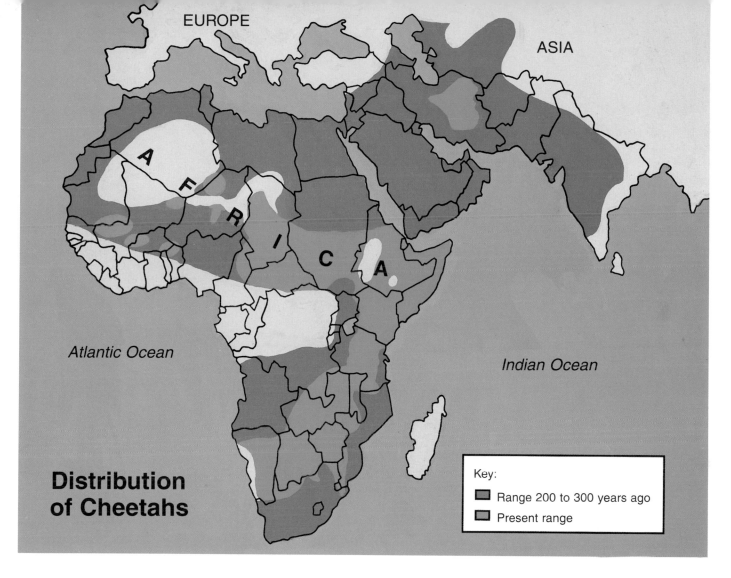

Distribution of Cheetahs

Key:
- ■ Range 200 to 300 years ago
- □ Present range

Akbar the Great, kept as many as 3,000 cheetahs for a sport called coursing. The cheetahs were trained to hunt animals in front of an audience. A blindfolded cheetah was taken to an open field where a gazelle was grazing. The blindfold was removed, and the cheetah bolted after the prey. The watching crowd cheered the cheetah's lightning speed as it chased down the gazelle.

One hundred years ago, over 100,000 cheetahs lived in Africa alone. As of the late 1990s, fewer than 10,000 remain, mostly in small areas of southern and eastern Africa. The problem is even more grim for Asia—fewer than 50 cheetahs can be found there. This fascinating animal is in serious danger of becoming **extinct,** or dying out.

THE ELEGANT CAT

The cheetah is bigger than a house cat but smaller than the big cats. Its coat is a light tan color with black spots. The pattern of spots is different for every cheetah. On its tail, the spots come together to form four to six rings. The tail ends in a bushy white tuft. Its belly is also white.

Cheetahs are easily recognized from other spotted cats by the long black stripes called **tear lines** that run from the corner of each eye down to the mouth. Scientists think these lines protect the cheetah's eyes from the glare of the sun. (Football players rub black grease under their eyes for the same effect.) Cheetahs hunt during the bright light of day and rely on their eyesight to find their prey.

The black tear lines under a cheetah's eyes help it see in bright sunlight.

A cheetah's mane is barely noticeable.

A cheetah's short fur looks as if it would be soft to the touch, but actually it feels like a coarse brush. The fur that makes up its black spots is longer and softer. Along the back of the neck, the fur forms a short **mane** a few inches long. Sometimes the male's mane is larger than the female's. However, it's still much shorter than a lion's mane and doesn't circle its whole head as a lion's does.

11

Cheetahs have small heads with short, rounded ears. Compared to big cats, cheetahs' chests are bigger in proportion to the rest of their bodies. Their legs are also much longer than those of other cats, and their bodies are leaner. An adult cheetah usually weighs between 100 and 140 pounds (45–64 kg). It stands about 30 inches tall (76 cm) at the shoulder and measures about 4 feet long (1.2 m). Its tail may be 26 to 33 inches long (66–84 cm). In comparison, a lion might weigh 500 pounds (227 kg) and be 9 feet long (2.7 m). Cheetah males are usually slightly bigger than females, but it is difficult to tell males and females apart.

Almost every part of a cheetah's body is made for speed. Its body is slender and light, and its long tail helps it stay balanced. The bones in a cheetah's feet and legs are especially designed to take the pounding of a hard run. Like other cats, they run on their toes. This makes it easier to make sudden turns.

Even the cheetah's claws are designed for speed. They are long, blunt, and very strong. The cheetah is the only member of the cat family whose claws can't retract, or pull up inside its paws. With the claws always pushed out, its paws look more like a dog's feet than a cat's. (Because of this, some people used to think cheetahs were part dog and part cat.) These special claws grip the ground and help the cheetah push off the same way a track shoe with cleats helps a runner start a race. From a standing start, the cheetah can reach 45 miles per hour (72 km/h) in 2 seconds. Most race cars cannot accelerate that fast.

Cheetahs cannot retract their claws the way house cats and big cats can.

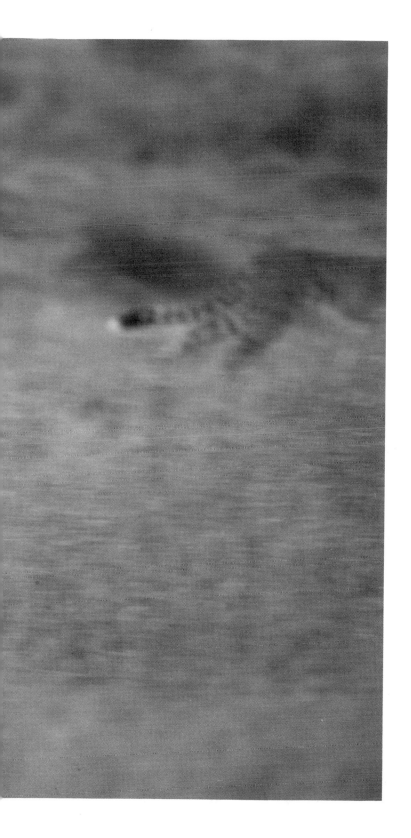

The cheetah's spine, or backbone, works somewhat like a toy Slinky to help the cat take long strides. As it runs, its spine bends and straightens, pushing the cheetah forward like a giant spring. For short distances, no animal can match the speed of a cheetah. It can cover as much as 20 feet (6 m) in one stride and reach speeds of up to 70 miles per hour (113 km/h). A racehorse at its fastest gallops just over 40 miles per hour (64 km/h). A sprinting cheetah looks as if it is flying across the ground rather than running.

A CHEETAH'S DAY

On a typical day, the cheetah wakes at sunrise. The animal stretches its long legs and then slowly stands, arching its back. After stretching, it sets off to look for prey. Climbing up on termite mounds or other small hills helps it get a clear view over the flat, grassy **savanna** where it lives. When a cheetah sits on its haunches and stares across the plain, its lean body resembles an Egyptian statue.

Keen eyesight helps cheetahs spot their prey from as far as 3 miles away (4.8 km). Like all cats, they are **carnivores,** or meat eaters. They hunt small- and medium-sized animals such as antelope, impalas, rabbits, game birds, and young ostriches. A small antelope called a Thomson's gazelle is their most common meal.

When the heat of the day becomes too much for a cheetah, it finds shade in which to rest. Even when it's very hot, cheetahs don't drink much water. They get most of their water from the meat they eat. On occasion, they drink from water holes or rivers, but amazingly, they can go for up to 10 days without water.

In late afternoon, after it has cooled down, the cheetah resumes its patrol. Unlike big cats, the cheetah is **diurnal,** or active during the day, so its nights are usually spent sleeping or resting in one place.

Resting in the shade (top) *and an occasional drink of water* (left) *help keep cheetahs cool.*

Cheetahs do not have a permanent home or den. Each year, most cheetahs migrate, or travel, over a large area, following grazing herds of gazelles, impalas, and other hoofed **mammals.** Cheetahs travel the same area year after year, covering as much as 40 square miles (64 km²). Females live alone except when they have babies, called **cubs.** If a female is walking across the plain and sees another female, she will turn her head and look the other way. They avoid all contact with one another.

Males live alone or with a small group called a **coalition.** Often the members of a coalition are brothers. Males in these groups are usually healthier than lone males, because they have more success at hunting. Two or more males hunting together are able to hunt larger prey such as young giraffes, buffalo calves, or zebras.

A female's only companions are her cubs (left), but a male sometimes lives with other males in a coalition (below).

Coalitions do not migrate. They choose an area, called a **territory,** to call home, and they hunt animals that wander into that area. To mark their territory, they spray urine on trees and rocks. The smell tells other male cheetahs to stay out. Males that dare to enter a coalition's territory are chased out or sometimes even attacked and killed. A female passing through the area is ignored unless she is ready to mate.

A male cheetah marks his territory.

THE SWIFT HUNTER

With its excellent eyesight, a cheetah spots its prey off in the distance. It lowers its head, a sign that the hunt is on. Now the cheetah moves slowly forward, keeping its head lowered and its eyes fixed on its prey. The cheetah's golden coat blends in with the tall grass. Sometimes the only clue that the cheetah is approaching is the white tuft on the end of its tail, which it holds high above the grass. If the animal it is stalking appears nervous or senses danger, the cheetah will freeze in place and remain still until the animal relaxes and begins to graze again.

Finally, when the cheetah is within 300 to 550 feet (92–168 m) of its prey—the length of one or two football fields—it springs into action. As the cat bounds through the grass, the startled animal begins to run. The cheetah is a blur of motion as it stretches out its long body and tail. Within seconds the cheetah catches up to the fleeing animal. With a front paw, it strikes the animal on the rump. On the inside of the cheetah's foreleg is a claw called a **dewclaw.** This sharp, curved claw hooks the victim and helps knock it over.

A dewclaw

The chase is on between a cheetah and a jackal.

As the animal crashes to the ground, the cheetah clamps its jaws down on the animal's throat, cutting off the air supply. The animal is often larger than the cheetah, but it doesn't even have time to struggle or kick the cheetah off. It is already gasping for breath from the chase, so in only a few seconds the animal stops breathing and dies. The whole hunt and kill may take as little as 20 seconds.

It's not hard for a cheetah to overpower a tired, winded Thomson's gazelle.

A Thomson's gazelle naturally turns and flees if it sees a cheetah approaching. It would be better off standing its ground.

The cheetah's speed makes it hard for an animal to get away. But surprisingly, the animal would have a better chance of surviving if it were to just stand still. Cheetahs hunt by singling out one animal and chasing it down. If the animal didn't run, it would have the strength to withstand a swipe on the rump and fight off the cheetah.

Still, cheetahs don't catch every animal they go after. Their speed makes them tire quickly, sometimes forcing them to give up on a long chase. They are successful only about half the time. However, cheetahs are more successful than big cats, who succeed only about one time out of three.

After the cheetah kills its prey, it drags the victim to an area hidden by bushes or trees. The cheetah doesn't want vultures or other predators to find the kill. Exhausted from the short but rapid chase, it sits and pants like a dog, its chest heaving with each breath. The cheetah will need 20 to 30 minutes to catch its breath before it can eat. Finally rested, the cheetah eats quickly, tearing off huge hunks of meat and gulping them down. Several times it will stop between bites and look around for other predators. If a mother and her cubs are eating together, they position themselves around the dead animal in a star formation. Each one can reach the kill without quarreling.

A cheetah stands over its prey, panting (inset), *until it is able to eat.*

Once this cheetah is full, it will simply walk away and leave the leftovers behind.

The eating habits of cheetahs are different from those of big cats. A cheetah gorges itself on its kill. When its stomach is full, the cheetah walks away, regardless of how much food remains. In contrast, lions guard their kill for several days. Tigers come back later for a second helping. Leopards drag their kill up into a tree for safekeeping and a mid-night snack. Cheetahs eat only fresh kill. And unlike the big cats, cheetahs rarely eat anything they haven't killed themselves. In one way, this behavior can help a cheetah survive. Humans sometimes use traps with meat as bait to catch wild animals. But cheetahs aren't tempted by an easy meal and ignore the bait.

Often before a cheetah has finished its meal, a lion or pack of hyenas will steal the cheetah's food. With weak jaws and blunt claws, the cheetah is not equipped to defend itself against more powerful animals. At first sight of a lion or hyena, it lowers its head and backs off. Even a group of vultures will scare a cheetah away. The cheetah's superior speed and hunting skills have produced dinner for another animal. The hungry cheetah will have to try again. It may have to hunt for 2 or 3 more days before making another kill. This is particularly hard for a mother trying to kill enough food to feed her cubs.

Cheetahs are rarely agressive toward other animals or each other. This gentle cat will give up its prey to these vultures before it gets into a fight.

26

FAMILY LIFE

Cheetahs mate and give birth to cubs throughout the year. There is not a special breeding season. Seven to fourteen days before the female is ready to mate, her urine takes on a special scent. When she urinates on trees and rocks in her area, she lets males know she will be ready to mate soon.

The time during which a female is able to mate, called **estrus,** lasts for 1 week. The **dominant** male in the area, who is larger and stronger than the other males, follows the scent and finds the female. The male and female sniff one another and stay together for a few hours or a day. When the female is ready, she allows the male to mount her.

After the cheetahs mate, the male leaves. If the female does not become pregnant, she will go into estrus again in 10 days. If she does become pregnant, her cubs will be born in about 3 months. When she is ready to give birth, she finds a quiet spot hidden by rocks or bushes. She lies down on her side, and the cubs are born. Males and females have no contact other than for mating. Males do not help raise or protect the cubs.

A male and a female check each other out before they mate.

A cheetah mother takes good care of her cubs. As soon as they are born, she nestles them close to her to keep them warm. The cubs are blind and helpless, but they are able to find their mother's nipples to nurse. Her milk is the cubs' first food.

Cheetahs may have one to eight cubs at a time (a group called a litter). The average litter is three or four. Newborns weigh from 8 to 10 ounces (227–284 g).

From the moment of birth, cubs face the constant threat of predators. Mother cheetahs have a big job trying to keep the cubs safe. Every 3 or 4 days, a mother will move her newborn litter to a new hiding spot. She carries each cub by the back of the neck, the same way a house cat carries her kittens. Predators are less likely to find the cubs by their scent if they have not been in the same spot for long. In a 6-week period, one observer noted that a mother cheetah moved her cubs 21 times. In spite of her protection, one cub was eaten by a leopard.

It's mealtime for these two cubs.

At 5 to 10 days old, the cubs open their eyes and begin to crawl around. Their mother calls them by making low, birdlike chirping sounds. The cubs answer with shrill, high-pitched chirps.

After 3 weeks, the cubs are able to walk and follow after their mother. While she is hunting, the cubs hide quietly nearby. Any noise would attract the attention of predators.

The heads, necks, and backs of the newborns are covered with a furry coat called a **mantle.** The mantle is about 3 inches long (7.5 cm) and is grayish white on the ends and black closer to the skin. The long hair makes the cubs look bigger and less helpless to predators. Their coloring may help them blend into the shadows. Some scientists think a cub's mantle **mimics,** or looks similar to, the honey badger, a fierce animal that most predators avoid. A predator who has had a run-in with a honey badger may think twice about preying on a cheetah cub.

When the cubs are between 8 and 12 weeks old, they begin to lose their black-and-white mantles. In a few months, they will have full, spotted coats. Their spotted coats help them blend into the tall grass, but cubs are still in constant danger from predators. Lions, hyenas, leopards, and other animals will eat the cubs if they have the chance.

This cub still sports a fuzzy mantle. As it grows older, the black-and-white mantle hairs will fall out and the spots on its legs will darken. The white fur on its belly won't change.

A cub practices pulling its dinner to safety. Most likely, its mother made the kill.

At about 2 weeks, tiny teeth grow in. At 4 weeks, the cubs begin to eat some meat that their mother brings to them. Their adult teeth will grow in at 10 to 14 months.

From about 6 months on, the cubs eat only meat. The mother tries to make one kill every day to feed them. As the cubs grow older, the mother teaches them how to hunt for themselves. At first they watch her. Later she will bring them small animals that are still alive. The cubs must learn exactly where to bite an animal's throat in order to kill it. If they miss the windpipe, the animal will get away, and it could harm them with its horns or hooves. It will be almost a year and a half before the cubs are able to hunt on their own.

When not learning how to hunt, cubs spend their days playing, chasing each other's tails, and stalking their mother's feet. They play like kittens, tumbling, wrestling, and rolling over and over in the grass. They pounce on one another in a cheetah game of leapfrog. This playing helps develop strong muscles and teaches them skills they will need to survive. Sometimes their mother joins in.

Playtime for a mother and her cub

Grooming or cleaning is an important part of a cheetah's life from an early age. Like all cats, cheetahs have long, rough tongues covered with tiny **rasps,** or hooks. When the cheetah licks its coat, the rasps comb through the hairs to remove dirt, grass, and loose fur. Cheetahs spend many hours every day grooming. A mother and her cubs help each other with the task. Particularly after eating, they all pitch in to make sure everyone's face is clean. At the same time, they purr noisily—almost like a house cat, but at a much greater volume! Their purring can be heard up to 20 feet away (6 m). Cheetahs purr loudest while grooming each other and while resting. Purring is a way of communicating coziness and friendship to one another.

Scientists don't really know how cats purr. They do know that cats have two sets of vocal chords. Each set produces different sounds. Scientists believe the purring sound is made when the blood flow increases near the upper vocal chords. The sound of the flowing blood is made louder by the air the cat is breathing in and out.

Cheetahs cannot roar, as big cats do. If a hyena or a human tries to steal her family's food or come close to her cubs, a female will moan and growl. She may also lunge forward and stamp her feet on the ground. She raises the hair on her shoulders and neck to make herself look larger. But all of this is a bluff to frighten the animal or person away from her cubs. Solitary cheetahs are usually gentle animals. However, male cheetahs in a coalition have been known to fight to the death an intruder who enters their territory.

Sometimes just pretending to be fierce is enough to scare away a creature that comes too close.

When the cubs are between 16 and 18 months old, the mother leaves to mate again and raise a new litter. She has protected her cubs and taught them as much as she can. Now they will have to survive on their own. The cubs stay together for a few more months. Then the females leave. The male cubs may remain together for life, or they too may strike out on their own.

The cubs are now able to mate. However, they usually wait until they are older. First-time mothers are usually 2 years old. Males might wait longer than 2 years if there are older and more dominant males in the area.

These cubs are nearly old enough to live on their own.

THE VANISHING CHEETAH

The future of cheetahs is uncertain. Humankind is running out of time to save these elegant cats. In the near future, there may no longer be any cheetahs left in the wild. The facts speak for themselves. Cheetahs are dying at a faster rate than they can be born. The present life span of a cheetah in the wild is a brief 7 years. Even though females breed frequently, only one in three cubs reaches the age of 2 years.

Fences built to protect farmers' crops and livestock are cutting up the open areas cheetahs need to catch their prey. A starving cheetah may settle for a meal of livestock, such as one of these cows, instead.

The greatest single threat to cheetah survival is loss of **habitat**—the savannas where they live. In countries where cheetahs live, the human population is exploding. In order to feed the growing numbers of people, more land is needed to grow crops for food. At an alarming pace, large areas of the savannas are being divided up and fenced off for farmland and pastures.

As farms are built, antelope, impalas, young ostriches, and other animals that make up the cheetah's diet are moving away. But cheetahs can't move with them. They need wide open areas to chase down their kill. So they stay on the savannas, where less food is available and there are more cheetahs and other predators competing for it. Cheetahs may hunt rabbits, birds, lizards, and frogs instead. They may also kill cattle and other farm animals. Understandably, this is hard on the farmers, and in some countries, they are allowed to shoot cheetahs to protect their livestock. This reduces the number of cheetahs even more.

Poachers, or illegal hunters, are another problem facing cheetahs. Poachers kill cheetahs and sell their skins at high prices. Most skins are made into expensive fur coats. Some people also hang cheetah skins on their walls for decoration or use them to cover pillows. As cheetahs become more scarce, their skins become more valuable. International laws are supposed to protect cheetahs, but hundreds of the cats still die this way each year.

To protect cheetahs from poachers, some areas have been set aside as wild animal parks, or **reserves.** Serengeti National Park and Masai Mara Game Reserve are parks in Tanzania and Kenya that are trying to help the plight of cheetahs. However, even on the reserves, cheetahs are not safe if there are large numbers of big cats, who eat cheetah cubs and steal cheetah kills. Cheetahs have always faced this risk. However, with the number of cheetahs and the amount of available food declining, the situation has become more serious.

A storm looms over Serengeti National Park.

A scientist at the San Diego Wild Animal Park studies a cheetah up close.

The future of cheetahs may be in zoos. In zoos, the cheetah's life span is between 12 and 17 years. If they lived that long in the wild, this would mean each female would be able to raise up to six litters of cubs over the course of her life.

But for cheetahs, life in zoos has been difficult too. Cheetahs do not breed well in captivity. Females do not come into estrus as often as they do in the wild. And scientists have discovered that 70 to 75 percent of the **sperm,** or male reproductive cells, are defective in males both in zoos and in the wild. This may prevent successful breeding. Occasionally, the cubs that are born are not well cared for by their mothers. Then the cubs must be hand-raised by humans, or they will die.

Prior to 1956, only one captive birth of a cheetah was recorded. Even Akbar the Great, who kept thousands of cheetahs, was unsuccessful at breeding these cats. As scientists learn more about cheetahs, more cubs are being born in captivity. But fewer than half of all zoos that have tried to breed cheetahs have succeeded.

There isn't much difference between the genes of these two cheetahs, whether they are related or not.

Why do they fail? To find the answer, scientists are studying how cheetahs live and reproduce in the wild. Increasingly, studies are focusing on **genes.** Genes are found in all cells. They serve as a pattern for any new cells that are made and determine everything about an animal—including its pattern of spots, size, personality, and general health—that makes it different from other cheetahs. Genes from both parents are passed on to their offspring.

Scientists have discovered that the genes of cheetahs in captivity and in the wild are almost identical. This means that there is no variation in the species, regardless of where the animal lives. Over 10,000 years ago, there were probably four different species of cheetahs. Then something caused almost all of the cheetahs to die. Three of the four species vanished completely. The cheetahs that still roam the earth are all descendant from a very small number of cheetahs. Because of this, less than 1 percent of a cheetah's genes are different from another cheetah. In contrast, other cats differ by 21 percent. Humans vary by 32 percent.

Variation is needed within a species to allow animals to grow stronger and avoid disease. The differences in genes allow some animals of a species to adapt, or change, to deal better with changes around them. For example, if the climate grows colder, animals with longer fur are more likely to survive—and raise more offspring. Those babies will have longer fur too, and so will *their* offspring. In another case, if a food source is taken away, animals might adapt by changing their eating habits. They will be more likely to survive and teach their young to eat these new foods than animals who don't change their eating habits and go hungry.

Animals that have similar genes tend to respond to changes around them in the same way. If one cheetah is unable to fight illness or adapt to a changing environment, it is likely many others won't either. Thus the species declines and becomes more vulnerable to disease.

In 1982, over half the cheetahs living in Wildlife Safari, an animal park in Oregon, died from a disease called feline infectious peritonitis. The animals did not have enough variation in their genes to allow them to adapt and resist the illness, and many died.

Veterinarians take sperm from a healthy male.

In the wild, females mate with the strongest and most dominant male. In zoos, there are fewer cheetahs and fewer choices. This is the greatest challenge for scientists trying to save the cats. Zoos in North America are working together to increase the cheetah's chances for survival. As part of the Species Survival Plan (SSP), zoos keep records of parents and their offspring. They want to breed animals that are as distantly related as possible, so that there will be more variation in the offspring's genes.

The SSP also makes sure the healthiest cheetahs mate with each other. Veterinarians and zookeepers pay close attention to the animals' diet, stress, and behavior. They watch carefully anything that can affect cheetahs' ability to reproduce and to live longer.

Several zoos have had some success. Both Wildlife Safari and the San Diego Wild Animal Park, in California, have had over 100 cheetahs born in their parks since 1970. Other successful breeding programs are located at the Columbus Zoo in Ohio, the St. Louis Zoo in Missouri, the White Oak Conservation Center in Florida, and Fossil Rim Wildlife Center in Texas. Scientists hope that someday some of the offspring of captive cheetahs can be returned to the wild, if there is any wilderness left.

To protect those cheetahs left in the wild, naturalists in Africa are working with farmers to find ways for the farmers to live peacefully with the cats. The naturalists are encouraging farmers to use dogs or donkeys, instead of guns, to scare off the cats and protect their cattle. Another option for farmers is to catch cheetahs rather than shoot them. In Namibia, the government moves these captured animals to reserves in other countries in southern Africa. The wild cheetahs are carefully checked out by veterinarians. If the males are strong and healthy, sperm is collected and sent to zoos in the United States to add variety to their breeding programs. Then the animals are returned to the reserves.

Some of these efforts are showing positive results. For the first time in many years, the cheetah population in Kenya seems to be holding steady. Scientists hope this trend will continue.

The vanishing cheetah is in its final race. But it is not racing against a gazelle or a wildebeest. This time it is racing against extinction. If the cheetah loses the race, then all of nature will feel the loss. Lions, leopards, hyenas, jackals, vultures, and other animals who depend on the hunting skills of the cheetah will suffer. Other species of animals and even plants will be affected.

We must find a way to halt the widespread destruction of savannas without denying countries their right to grow food. Cheetahs must be protected until scientists can help this declining species grow strong once more. Governments, scientists, zoos, and people everywhere working together can help this magnificent cat win the race. When future generations see a golden streak sprinting across the savanna, they will know it is the cheetah, the fastest animal on land.

GLOSSARY

carnivore: an animal that eats meat

coalition: a small group of two to four male cheetahs—often brothers—that live together

cub: a baby cheetah

dewclaw: a long, curved claw on the inside of the foreleg that is used to help hook and knock over prey

diurnal: active during the day

dominant: the strongest and most powerful in an area

estrus: a week-long period during which a female cheetah is able to become pregnant

extinct: having no members of a species left alive

genes: tiny units in the cells of living things that determine the characteristics that offspring will inherit from their parents

habitat: the type of environment in which an animal lives

mammals: animals with hair or fur that produce milk to feed their young

mane: a section of longer fur on the back of the neck

mantle: a furry, grayish white and black coat that grows on a cub's head, neck, and back

mimic: to develop the coloring, habits, or body structure of another species

rasps: tiny hooks on a cat's tongue

reserve: a piece of land set aside for wildlife and off-limits to hunters

savanna: a flat, grassy area in a hot, dry climate

sperm: male reproductive cells

tear lines: dark lines in a cheetah's fur that run from the inner edge of its eyes down to the corners of its mouth

territory: an area claimed as one's home and defended from other animals

INDEX

Additional photos courtesy of: © Konrad Wothe/Ellis Nature Photography, p. 8 (bottom left); © Richard Hewett, pp. 13, 21 (top); © Tony Heald-BBC/Ellis Nature Photography, pp. 16 (top left), 21 (bottom), 34, 35; © Ron O'Connor-BBC/Ellis Nature Photography, p. 19; © Keith Scholey-BBC/Ellis Nature Photography, pp. 26, 28–29, 32; © John Downer-BBC/Ellis Nature Photography, p. 30; © Bernard Castelein-BBC/Ellis Nature Photography, p. 31; Visuals Unlimited/© Sylvan Wittwer, p. 37; © Zoological Society of San Diego/Ron Garrison, pp. 39, 42. Map on page 9 by John Erste.

ABOUT THE AUTHOR

Dianne M. MacMillan has always been fascinated by cheetahs' speed and elegance, and their long association with humans. She hopes that this book can help turn the tide away from extinction by encouraging young readers to continue the fight for species survival. Ms. MacMillan is a former elementary school teacher with numerous children's books and magazine articles to her credit, including *Elephants: Our Last Land Giants,* another Carolrhoda Nature Watch Book. She lives in Orange, California, with her husband, her youngest daughter, and their dog and cat.

ABOUT THE PHOTOGRAPHER

Gerry Ellis has explored the world as a professional photographer and naturalist for nearly two decades. His images of wildlife and natural landscapes have won him many awards, including several honors in the BBC Wildlife Photographer of the Year competition. Among his many publications is *Rhinos,* also from Carolrhoda. Mr. Ellis lives in Portland, Oregon.